The Art of Chinese Pavilions

Ⓦ Foreign Languages Press   Beijing

"Culture of China" Editorial Board:

Consultants: Cai Mingzhao, Zhao Changqian, Huang Youyi and Liu Zhibin
Chief Editor: Xiao Xiaoming
Board Members: Xiao Xiaoming, Li Zhenguo, Tian Hui, Fang Yongming, Hu Baomin, Hu Kaimin, Cui Lili and Lan Peijin

Written by: Zhu Junzhen
Photographer: Zhu Junzhen

Chinese Text Editor: Wang Zhi
Translated by: Xiong Zhenru, Ouyang Weiping, Wang Qin, Kuang Peihua
English Text Editor: He Jun
Designed by: Wang Zhi

First Edition 2002

The Art of Chinese Pavilions

ISBN 7-119-03118-X

© Foreign Languages Press
Published by Foreign Languages Press
24 Baiwanzhuang Road, Beijing 100037, China
Home Page: http://www.flp.com.cn
E-mail Addresses: info@flp.com.cn
                              sales@flp.com.cn

The Art of Chinese Pavilions

The pillars of the road pavilion are tree trunks.

Contents

I. A Brief Introduction to the History of Chinese Pavilions

I. A Brief Introduction to the History of Chinese Pavilions

Pavilions, seen everywhere in the vast land of China, are small buildings closely connected with people's lives in sightseeing and leisure. Pavilions have many functions and different artistic shapes, and they have become an integral feature of both natural scenic spots and man-made parks or gardens. In China, they are so ubiquitous that it is said, "There is no famous mountain without a pavilion," "no rivers or lakes without pavilions," and "no parks or gardens without pavilions." In a park or garden, other buildings might be dispensable, but not pavilions. So, from ancient times to today, pavilions have been associated with parks or gardens.

Multipurpose pavilions may serve as a place for viewing scenery or resting. Their great variety of designs and styles are a reflection of the Chinese culture. Pavilions cover very little land area and come in many styles; thus they are easy and inexpensive to build. However, the decision to build, the choice of a site, the naming of the pavilion, and the couplets hanging there, all reveal much about the spiritual world of the builder. Chinese garden architecture thus concisely captures a great deal of meaning and charm.

Pavilions date at least back to the Spring and Autumn and Warring States Period two thousand years ago, when Fu Chai, the king of Wu, built Wutong and Huijing Gardens, in which "pavilions were constructed and bridges were built." In ancient times, when a garden was built, people dug ponds, made hills and built terraces and pavilions. They first built a hill or a terrace, on top of which a pavilion then was constructed. In a pavilion, one could gaze off into the distance, rest or seek shelter from the rain. The pavilions built in this period already visually resembled modern ones.

In the Qin Dynasty alone, more than 300 large and small imperial palaces were built. They were either "provisional imperial palaces and connected halls facing one another" or "building complexes with halls lying in every five paces and pavilions in every ten paces." Unfortunately, no writings have been found so far to describe such pavilions directly. The construction of imperial gardens in the Han Dynasty followed the example of the Qin. But "The List of a Hundred Officials and Townships" in the book *History of Han* records: "Generally there is a 'ting' (pavilion) every ten *li*, and ten 'pavilions' form a township." Obviously, in the Han Dynasty, "pavilion" was the title of the administrative unit beneath the township. Tradition has it that Liu Bang, the founding emperor of the Han Dynasty, once held the minor official post, "Head of Sishang Pavilion."

Besides, the pavilion was also used as a unit of measurement. A "far pavilion" marked every ten *li* (a unit of measurement of 500 meters) and a "near pavilion" every five *li*. Travelers or the general public used these pavilions as a place to rest, dine, lodge, or hold farewell parties. Tang Dynasty poet Li Bai nostalgically describes the pavilions:

Jade-like stairs stand empty and quiet;
Evening birds are flying quickly in return.
Where are they returning to?
None other than distant or near pavilions.

Pavilions continued to serve these functions through the later dynasties. Celebrated Yuan Dynasty dramatist Wang Shifu's famous scene in his masterpiece *West Chamber* has the main character, Mistress Cui Yingying, giving an affectionate sendoff to her lover Zhang Sheng in the ten-*li* "distant pavilion."

The sendoff is a custom of the Chinese people. It was particularly popular in ancient times when, without convenient transportation, the pavilion was the natural place for people to see off their loved ones. When a farewell took place in a pavilion, scholars would often write poems to express their sorrow and sadness at parting. A very typical example was Li Bai, who wrote many poems in this vein. The following three poems of his show the close relationship between the sendoff and pavilions:

Laolao Pavilion
The place that breaks my heart in the world
Is the pavilion called Laolao Pavilion;
Even the spring wind knows the sadness of parting,
So it is reluctant to turn willow branches green.

In this poem the sendoff pavilion refers to the place for "expressing grief and sadness at parting". "Laolao" signifies a newly built pavilion. The last two lines of the poem tell us about the ancient custom of breaking off a willow branch to give to friends when parting in spring.

Xiexin Pavilion
Xie Pavilion is the place to part;
Sadness rises at the sight of the scenery.
After guests are gone, only the moon hangs in the sky;
A blue river runs in solitude around the empty mountains.
The sun shines over the pond flowers in spring,
Cicadae sing at night outside the bamboo window in autumn.
The present and the past all are the same;
Deep songs are always sung for old friends.

Xie Pavilion, located to the north of Xuancheng in present-day Anhui Province, was the place where Xie Tiao, a poet of the Southern Dynasties, sent off friends. Li Bai admired Xie Tiao's poetry, and he wrote the above poem to express the feelings he shared with Xie Tiao in sending off friends.

At the Farewell for Du Buque and Fan Shixiang in Autumn at Lujunyaoci Pavilion
... The white jade pot is filled with wine from Lu,
Golden bridles are taken off for the farewell.
Saddles, removed, rest by an ancient tree,
Bands, untied, hang on horizontal branches.
Songs and drums are heard from the pavilion by the river,
Sweet melodies are drifting fast along the wind ...

Li Bai wrote this poem at a farewell party for two friends, conjuring up a moving scene: After dismounting from horseback, a group of people go to rest by an ancient tree. They undo their bands, hang their saddles on the tree and then come to a pavilion to play musical instruments and sing songs. The melodies they produce are so strong and powerful that they seem to give courage to those to leave and drive away the sorrows at parting. From this poem, we can see that the pavilion was also a place where people played music at farewell in ancient times.

In addition to sendoff pavilions along the roadside,

there were also sendoff pavilions built in private building compounds or courtyards, as in *Note of Lingdong Mountain House* written by a Minister of Punishments of the Ming Dynasty, the poet and scholar Wang Shizhen: "When old friends pass by my place, they usually don't wear hats but towels on their heads. They are treated with wine; tea made of spring water; and vegetables, bamboo shoots, taro, and millet grown in the fields. If they want to stay, they are put up in the chambers; if they want to leave, I give them a sendoff in the pavilion. I share my residence with my guests." When guests wanted to leave after a happy get-together at his home, the host would walk them to the courtyard. He would stop at the pavilion and would not go any farther. The pavilion referred to here was a place to send off frequent guests, not like the above-mentioned sendoff pavilions in the open countryside.

In addition to pavilions used to hold farewell for guest, pavilions were also used to express sad feelings at parting. It was a common practice to build pavilions for cherishing special feelings in ancient times. Today, in Cangbo Township in Yongjia County of present-day Zhejiang Province there are two famous, well-preserved pavilions: "Looking Forward to Elder Brother" and "Sending off Younger Brother." The story about how the two brothers lovingly cared for each other and mutually declined modestly to inherit the family property is still very popular in the area.

In the Han Dynasty there appeared "pavilion barricades." The "Life of Wang Ju" in the *History of Eastern Han* records: "Wang Ju and Du Mao were called to build pavilion barricades by piling up stones and earth along Feigu Road for over three hundred *li*." Hence the Chinese saying: "Pavilion barricades run alongside the Yellow River." In a passage called "Soul" from the book *Strategies of the Warring States*, it says: "Soldiers were sent to do defense on four sides. Many of them went to safeguard pavilion barricades. Water transports for grain and granaries amounted to 100,000." It is clear that pavilion barricades became a kind of border fortress from the

Warring States period onward. Besides simple pavilions, there were also "pavilion forts" (ancient watchtowers) and "pavilion beacons" (beacon towers at the border).

During the Jin Dynasty, because of the influence of religion and metaphysics, there was a reemphasis on nature and the recovery of original purity and simplicity. Thus, many people began to build natural landscape parks and gardens. Consequently there emerged many temple and monastery gardens and natural scenic spots, in which pavilions became a must. Pavilions built for the purpose of drinking wine, composing poems, and playing music were called "Orchid Towers." Orchid Towers became rampant in the Jin although they were first developed in the Han. Scholars like the great writer Wang Xizhi of the Jin came to "gather at new pavilions to hold parties on fine days." They took baths and made sacrifices in the wilderness, leaving many romantic stories and adding to pavilions a strong cultural flavor.

After the Sui Dynasty unified the Northern and Southern

I-1An imitation of an ancient Han Dynasty style (206 B.C. - A.D.220) pavilion in Guangzhou

Dynasties and moved the capital to Luoyang, the huge Xiyuan Park was built. The park's Xiaoyao Pavilion was unprecedented in structure and size. Perhaps this was the beginning of pavilions in imperial parks. By this time, pavilion began to play a greater role as a landscape attraction.

However, after the pavilion was regarded as a measuring unit, its function was broadened to serve as a "post." This can be verified by the ancient post tower left in Hengkuang Township near Suzhou by the side of the Grand Canal dug in the Sui Dynasty (see illustration I-2).

Located at the confluence of the Grand Canal and Suzhou's Xu River, this ancient post pavilion is connected by a dyke and a rainbow bridge. In the shape of a rectangle, it has four stone pillars and two wood pillars, six beams, nine ridges, a tiled roof and brick walls, two doors to the north and south and two windows to the east and west. The place is the site of an ancient post pavilion. Posts were used to deliver official letters, pass on information to frontier troops, or provide transportation and accommodations for passing officials. This pavilion, first built in the Ming and rebuilt in the Qing, has a couplet written on its two pillars, which reads:

Guests, upon arrival, have food, tea and lodging at this makeshift home;
Lamps, hung high to wait for the moon on the post, reflect in the distant Xu River.

This couplet not only tells the functions of the pavilion but also serves as a relic of the postal system in the two thousand years from ancient time to the Qing Period.

During the prosperity of the Tang Dynasty, the building of both imperial gardens and private gardens of the common people reached a new high point. Garden pavilions surpassed the previous dynasties both in number and variety.

I-2 An ancient post pavilion in Hengkuang Township

In the three gardens (West Garden, East Inner Garden, and the Forbidden Garden) within the palace city, different kinds of pavilions were built.

In the Tang Dynasty there was also a popular ball game. A ball-field pavilion was built in the West Garden, Taiye Pavilion was built in the East Inner Garden, and another 24 pavilions were built in the Forbidden Garden.

As for the types of pavilions, in addition to Qushuiliubei Pavilion from the Jin, there appeared a kind of pavilion called "Rain Tower." When it rained, water came down from the roof on four sides to form a water curtain. They enjoyed watching the water falling from the eaves. To the east of the Dragon Pool within Xingqing Palace in Chang'an, the capital of the Tang, was built a square pavilion with double eaves and pointed roof, called "Chenxiang Pavilion." As a center of the building complex, the pavilion was surrounded by different kinds of peonies. Famous both for the sumptuous flowers it possessed and the precious wood it was built of, it was the first luxury pavilions. From the Tang Dynasty murals at Mogao Grottoes in Dunhuang, different types of pavilions can be found: square, hexangular, octagonal, round, tapered roof, gabled roof, double eaves, etc.

The Tang Dynasty natural landscape parks of scholars had an even greater variety of pavilions, with stress laid on the choice of site and cultural value. A fine example of this is Juyuanchi Park in Jiangshou, Shanxi Province, first built in the period between the Sui and Tang and rebuilt in the Ming. It is the oldest park in China. Most of it was destroyed; only its site remained. Today, some parts of it have been restored. In the park, a pavilion was built in the middle of a pond, and lotus flowers grow in the pond. On the pillars of the pavilion is written a couplet, which reads:

Walk through the winding path quickly; a shower of rain turns poplar and willow trees green;
Roll up the sparse curtain quietly; the fragrance of lotus flowers drift along the breeze over half the pond.

This couplet gives a vivid description of the park in spring and summer. There is another pavilion called

"Humble Tower" with stone tables and stools inside it. It also has a couplet:

Laugh at the thatched tower filled with some kind of unrefined and poor taste;
See beside the fine timbers and rocks lies a vast stretch of autumn water.

Besides these, there are many other pavilions such as Moon Viewing Pavilion, Cypress Pavilion, Semi-Circle Pavilion and New Pavilion. Some show scenes of the four seasons, some represent the mood of the park's owners, while others are used to entertain guests and rest. Obviously, pavilions play an important role in the park culture.

As time went by, pavilions became more and more exquisite. This is clearly seen from the description about the East Pavilion in "Note on the Eight Pavilions in Liuzhou" by the Tang Dynasty writer Liu Zongyuan: "The pavilion faces the river, with a forest of trees (pine, cypress, Chinese juniper, China fir, etc.) at its back and buildings beside it. In the front stretch two wings, which block off the view of the two sides of the surface of the river that can be taken from the facade of the pavilion. It produces the effect of 'turning the river into a lake.'" This example shows how a pavilion was cleverly designed by using specific topographical features.

The imperial gardens of the Song Dynasty were exemplified by Genyue Park on Longevity Hill in Bianjing (present-day Kaifeng). It was a large park, with "rocks piled into a hill, ponds dug into lakes, pavilions built on leveled rock ridges, and hills made for growing apricot trees." Numerous pavilions were built in the park. According to historical record, on the main and highest peak was Jieting Pavilion, on the second high peak was Clouds-Gathering Pavilion. On rocks on the mountain ridges were Jimu Pavilion, Xiaosen Pavilion, Luyun Pavilion, Banshan Pavilion, Chenglan Pavilion, Kunyun Pavilion, Tuanshan Pavilion, Yongyong Pavilion and Longyin Pavilion. On islets in the lake were Fuyang

Pavilion, Xuelang Pavilion and Huiyu Pavilion, and on level ground were Feiling Pavilion and other similar buildings. From the locations of these pavilions, we can see that they were ingeniously built for the purpose of enjoying natural scenery.

In modern Kaifeng, Dragon Pavilion is located on a high point 26 meters above the city ground. As the site of the palace garden of the Northern Song Dynasty with many cultural relics, it has become the symbol of Kaifeng. Originally, it was a wooden tower built on Coal Hill in the 31st year of the Kangxi Reign in the Qing Dynasty. Because the tablets of deceased emperors were enshrined in it, it was called Dragon Pavilion, and high officials came to pay homage to it during festivals. In the 12th year of the Yongzheng Reign (1734), a hall (the Longevity Hall) was built there, and the Dragon Pavilion was enlarged into a huge palace. So the present building is not the original Song Dynasty tower, although the site is. (I-3)

During the Song Dynasty, Luoyang was famous for its private gardens. According to Li Gefei's *Famous Gardens in Luoyang,* people built huge pavilions in their private gardens to overlook other gardens and thus borrow scenes from outside. This was because most of the private gardens were small in size and the scenes inside the gardens were limited. Congchun Pavilion in Congchun Garden, for example, was much taller than the surroundings, where people could "ascend at night to listen to the gurgling water of the Luo River in winter." In this period there appeared an important feature in the building of pavilions: group pavilions. For example, in the bamboo grove in Fuzheng Park were built five pavilions: Congyu, Pifeng, Yilan, Jiazhu and Jianshan, and in Renfeng Park of the Li Family were also five pavilions. The group form of five pavilions which became popular in later dynasties may have begun in this period.

But very few Song Dynasty pavilions are left today. Only Shaoxing's Shenyuan, a garden in commemoration of the Song Dynasty patriotic poet Lu You, has been restored. It represents the tragic love of "The Phoenix Hairpin," a much-admired classical poem. This small garden, covering an area of less than one hectare, has kept its original Song style. The two well pavilions of the garden are imitations of the Song style. Because the two wells were dug in the Song Dynasty, the two pavilions

I-4 An imitation of a Song Dynasty (960 - 1279) style well pavilion—the Hexagon Pavilion in the Shen Family Garden, Shaoxing

I-5 The ancient Yuan Dynasty (1279 - 1368) style pavilion in Baotou

were built to protect them. One pavilion is hexagonal (I-4) and has a caisson ceiling and skylight, while the other is rectangular and has a wooden fence around the well. The rectangular one is pervaded by an air of primitive simplicity and known as "The Well Tower of Six Dynasties."

The building of palaces and gardens of the Jin and Yuan Dynasties followed the example of the Northern Song, and a large number of pavilions were built in the imperial and private gardens in Beijing. But the most typical pavilion still extant is the octagonal pavilion with a tapered-roof in Baotou, which was first built in the Yuan Dynasty and repaired later. Its size and shape represent the bold and unrestricted architectural style of the nomadic tribes in the north. (I-5)

With the development of the architectural art, the pavilion began to have a greater ornamental function and was more and more tinged with the color of literature. Literary works depicting pavilions increased rapidly from the Tang and Song dynasties onward, and there appeared many literary masterpieces, such as "Note on the Eight Pavilions in Liuzhou" by Tang Dynasty writer Liu Zongyuan, "Note on Canglang Pavilion" by Su Shunqin, "Pavilion of the Drunken" by Ouyang Xiu, "Jiuqu Pavilion of Wuchang" by Su Zhe of the Song Dynasty, and "Flying-Spring Pavilion of Xiajiang Temple" by Yuan Mei of the Qing Dynasty. Pavilion inscriptions and couplets were seen everywhere. These developments enhanced the national distinctiveness of the Chinese pavilion culture, which was to develop further in the Ming and Qing dynasties.

Ji Cheng, a Ming Dynasty garden-building specialist, wrote a brilliant exposition in his book *Garden Art* about the implications and forms of pavilions as well as the choice of sites. According to him, pavilions are buildings for people to visit or rest in. Pavilions may be in the forms of a triangle, square, pentagon, hexagon, octagon, cross, plum blossom, and fan shape, among others. Pavilions should be built flexibly in accordance with local conditions. There are no fixed standards or regular patterns for pavilion building. Good sites for pavilions, in addition to rivers and lakes, also included streams, bamboo groves, mountaintops, valleys, and slopes. Pavilions can also be built over the stretches of water, or in caves. *Garden Art* forms the initial theory of pavilion building.

In the classic Qing Dynasty novel *A Dream of Red Mansions*, the descriptions of pavilion naming and enjoying scenery in pavilions reached consummation. In the Qing Dynasty, Chinese gardening reached a period of maturity and great prosperity, and pavilions in parks or gardens attained a high degree of artistic depth and width in terms of form, structure, layout, function, and cultural implication. In extant Ming and Qing parks or gardens, no matter whether imperial or private, natural places of historical interest and scenic beauty or famous religious mountains, we find pavilions everywhere. Around West Lake in Hangzhou there are over 100 pavilions; in the Summer Resort in Chengde, the largest extant imperial park in China, there are about 70 pavilions; and in the Summer Palace there are more than 50 pavilions.

I-6b Guanshengyi Pavilion in the Summer Palace, Beijing

-6a Double-eave pavilion in
he Summer Palace, Beijing

I-6e Twin pavilions in the Summer Palace, Beijing

I-7a Kuoru Pavilion on the bank of the Kunming Lake in the Summer Palace, Beijing

I-7b Xingqiao Pavilion on the bank of the Kunming Lake in the Summer Palace, Beijing

The Summer Palace, the last remaining imperial park of "The Three Hills and Five Parks" in the western suburbs of Beijing, is representative of the traditional Chinese gardening art at its peak, the cream of traditional garden building. The various exquisitely built pavilions in it are the flower of Chinese landscape gardening. (I-6a, b, c)

Built in the Qing Dynasty, the Summer Palace is the most complete well-preserved imperial park in China, with over 50 pavilions. Most of the pavilions are concentrated on the southern slope of Longevity Hill, Kunming Lake, and the Garden of Harmonious Pleasures on the eastern side (I-7a,b), although some pavilions stand facing the water at the West Dyke and eastern bank of Kunming Lake. The 50-odd pavilions have a unified style, with a wooden structure and a tapered glazed tile roof,

I-8a The Lama Pavilion on the Back Hill
around Sea-of-Wisdom in the Summer Palace

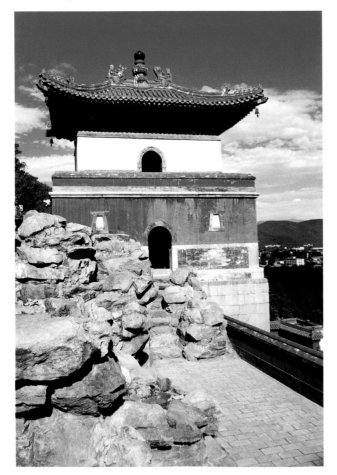

I-8b The Tibetan-style High Terrace
and False Window Pavilion

I-9b Front view of the Pavilion of
Blessed Shade in the Summer Palace

but are different in shape, size and layout. But some of the pavilions around Sea-of-Wisdom Temple are Tibetan in style (I-8a,b), and the Pavilion of Blessed Shade halfway up the hill is in the style of folk buildings of the Manchu Nationality (I-9a,b). All the pavilions in the Summer Palace have strong cultural connotations, and each

has a poetic name, meaningful inscriptions, and couplets. Yichiyunzai Pavilion, for example, takes its name from the poem "River Tower" by the Tang Dynasty poet Du Fu: "The river runs by fast but my mind remains quiet / As I don't aspire to the clouds high in the sky," while the name of Guanshengyi Pavilion comes from Pi Rixiu's poem: "Emotions rise instantly on hearing the whispering of the wind in the pines; / Feelings flow at the sight of the moon reflected in the stream." Kuoru Pavilion on the eastern bank of Kunming Lake fully expresses the aspiration and interest of past emperors, and it takes its name from a line of Sun Chou's poem "Visiting Tiantai Mountain": "So vast and boundless is the great void." In the early period there was no surrounding wall on the southeastern side of the pavilion, the place was very open and wide, with vast paddy fields and the mirror-like Kunming Lake setting each other off. The view became more beautiful when the pavilion, the largest of the whole park, was added. With the bronze ox and the beautiful Seventeen-Arch Bridge lying close by, the place turns

I-10a A panoramic view of the Orchid Pavilion in the Garden of Harmonious Pleasures in the Summer Palace

into a combination of pavilion, islet, and bridge, a most attractive scenic spot in the Summer Palace.

But the attraction with the greatest literary flavor in the Summer Palace is the Orchid Pavilion (I-10a,b) of the Garden of Harmonious Pleasures. Inside it stands a stone tablet, on the front side of which are carved the words "Looking for a Poem Path" and on the other three sides are carved lyric poems. Both the inscription and the poems are in the handwriting of the Qing Dynasty Emperor Qianlong, who profoundly understood traditional Chinese culture and gardening art. During his lifetime, he wrote inscriptions for many parks and gardens, which have become a part of the Chinese cultural heritage.

In a word, the pavilions in the Summer Palace are not only large in number but also varied in type. As representatives of pavilion building of the Qing Dynasty, they demonstrate the features of Chinese pavilion art in a period of great prosperity.

I-10b Front view of the Orchid Pavilion in the Garden of Harmonious Pleasures in the Summer Palace

I-10c The Double-Eave Round Pavilion in the Garden of Harmonious Pleasures in the Summer Palace

II. Types of Pavilions

Pavilions are related to people's lives in many ways, and thus there are many types and many means of classification. Some classifications are based on location, some on form, and others on materials used in building. In this album, Chinese pavilions are classified into the following seven types on the basis of function as well as features.

1. Pavilions for Resting

The famous Ming Dynasty book *Garden Art* defines pavilions in a section called "Explanations of Names": "Pavilion means a place where travelers may stop and rest." The Tang Dynasty scholar Sikong Tu went into seclusion on Mount Zhongtiao. He built a pavilion there, calling it "Resting Pavilion." Clearly, the primary function of pavilions is for resting.

Travelers, particularly those on long journeys, need places to rest en route and replenish drinking water supplies. As a result, road and tea pavilions appeared. During rain, pavilions keep travelers dry; during bright sunshine, travelers need a place to cool down. This is the origin of pavilions for shelter from rain or sun.

In the West Hill Scenic Area in Hangzhou, there is a tranquil natural forest with a small pavilion. The forest makes a whistling sound in the wind that the people found refreshing and pleasant. The pavilion is called the "Pleasant Whistling Pavilion." It contains a couplet:

The old and the new should each be half,
High mountains and flat ridges are good sites for pavilions.

The couplet beautifully describes the location and nature of road pavilions.

II-1-1b A resting pavilion hidden in the forest

In ancient times, road pavilions were tea-stalls, set up for passersby to rest and drink tea. Today, in Lishuiqiao Township, Yongjia County in southern Zhejiang, there is a tea pavilion from the Ming and Qing dynasties. Located by a crossroad on a hill beside a small river, the pavilion is attached to a building on two sides. Inside the pavilion, "Beautiful Woman" seats line three sides, with a small tea boiler in a corner. On the beams of the pavilion are pasted small red sheets with the names of those who have come to present tea on that day of that month. It is a custom among the local people to provide tea to passersby free of charge. This quaint practice is a local tradition from the Ming Dynasty.

Tea requires water for brewing, and thus most tea pavilions are built near rivers, wells, and springs. Hangzhou's famous Longjing tea has a special flavor because it is watered with water from Tiger-Dug Spring. A Tang Dynasty couplet describes the brewing of tea: "Bamboo grows on the bank of the fragrant lotus flower pond; / Tea is brewed with spring water with the shadows of jumping frogs." This description shows the close relations between tea and springs, although that poem refers specifically to the pavilion of China's "Tea Master"

Lu Yu and the Literature Spring located to the north of Tianmen, Hubei Province. At the southeastern side of Lu Yu Pavilion, the Literature Spring is in the shape of the character "品". Tradition has it that when Lu Yu was young, he brewed tea with the water from the spring for his master. Later, the prefect of Tianmen County built a pavilion and erected a stone tablet beside it. On one side of the stone tablet is the inscription "Literature Spring" and on the other side, "The True Place for Brewing Tea" with a small portrait of Lu Yu.

Some well pavilions are also tea-stalls. Beneath the sheer cliff half way up Mount Xiling about ten kilometers to the northwest of Yichang City, Hubei Province, stands a pavilion with a spring well. The clear water in the well resembles a mirror, and it never dries up. The local people call it "Divine Water." The famous Song Dynasty poet Lu You once visited it. When he saw the clear water, he made tea with it and wrote a poem on the cliff to praise the quality of the water. Since then the well has been called "Lu You Well," and a pavilion was built to cover it.

Although most road pavilions, tea pavilions, and pavilions for shelter from rain and sun are located by roads or water, their scenic function is not neglected. When a

pavilion is built, its location must be in a scenic place, and its design and shape must be harmonious with the surroundings. The pavilion and natural scenery together form a view. This was already stressed as early as in the Song Dynasty when Gushan Road was built at West Lake in Hangzhou. A poem describes the view: "The place is made up so beautifully by the scenery; / Three pavilions stand amidst fragrant lotus flowers." The road was built with the main attraction of the pavilion.

Pavilions for resting must have "benches to sit," "views to enjoy," and "tea to drink," in addition to their own scenic roles in the view.

II-1-3a The pavilion with "beautiful woman" seats

II-1-3b A resting pavilion in a traditional house

II-1-3c A resting pavilion with stone seats and tables

*II-1-3d A resting pavilion with stone
seats and tables and a weeping vine*

II-1-5a A simple resting pavilion

II-1-5b A simple resting pavilion

2. Pavilions for Viewing Scenery

Pavilions were incorporated into gardens as attractions for the first time in the Jin Dynasty. In natural landscape parks or gardens, the pavilion, because of its small size, flexible layout, varied structure and rich color, is an indispensable and attractive building for the man-made or natural surroundings. When well integrated with the hills, rocks, ponds, plants, and topography, the pavilion produces its own unique beauty of combining buildings with nature.

From a pavilion, one can see different views; listen to the sound of running water; hear the roar of waves; enjoy mountain scenes, grotesquely shaped rocks, plants and flowers, the moon, the sunrise and sunset. Pavilions provide a beautiful, comfortable and refreshing atmosphere. Moreover, most pavilions have inscriptions, paintings, poems, and couplets in them; this creates cultural interest.

Generally, the pavilions for viewing scenes are closely integrated with mountains, bodies of water, and forests. When a pavilion is built, it must be harmonious with the surroundings not only in shape, proportion and color but also in location. It must be a scene itself and a place to enjoy other scenes. Here are a few examples:

II-2-1a A simple, isolated mountaintop pavilion

(1) Mountain Pavilions

Most mountain pavilions are integrated into forests. It is no good for a pavilion to stand on a mountaintop solitarily or to be concealed in a forest completely. Because the pavilion on the mountaintop is a sign of the scenic spot concerned, so it must be "revealed" to some extent. But if it is revealed entirely, without anything nearby, it looks lonely and isolated just like the picture II-2-1a. If there are one or two trees next to it, it forms a scene (II-2-1b). The picture (II-2-1c) shows a twin-pavilion on a small peak in the mountains. It has two pine trees facing it on its southeastern side. The pavilion and the trees set one another off in the distance. When one enjoys the mountain views from the pavilion, the trees, far from blocking the vision, enhance the position of the pavilion.

II-2-1b Ancient pines next to a mountaintop pavilion

II-2-1c The mountaintop Twin Pavilion with two pine trees

II-2-2b A pavilion hidden in the forest

Pavilions halfway up the mountain are generally hidden in the forest. Mountain paths lead the way for people to rest, enjoy the scenery, watch waterfalls and springs, or look at flowers and plants (II-2-2a,b). Flowers and trees mostly surround pavilions that lie at the foot of mountains. The huge imperial tablet pavilion at the foot of Mount Tianping stands amidst a large stretch of Chinese sweet gum trees. This octagonal, double-eave pavilion was built when Emperor Qianlong of the Qing Dynasty visited Mount Tianping. On the four sides of the stone tablet inside the pavilion are engraved four poems written by Emperor Qianlong during his four visits to Mount Tianping (II-2-3).

In small gardens, mountain pavilions are built on man-made hills and are small in size. The smallest pavilions only cover an area of two or three square meters (II-2-4a,b). Some pavilions are even built on man-made mounds (II-2-4c), for elevation and to increase variation within the garden. Around such pavilions, small flowers or shrubs are planted.

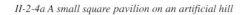

*II-2-3 The Imperial Tablet Pavilion at
the foot of Mount Tianping in Suzhou*

II-2-4b A small triangular pavilion on an artificial hill

II-2-4c A pavilion on a man-made terrace

(2) Water Pavilions

"Building pavilions by water" is a traditional motif in Chinese gardening. Water has greater flexibility than mountains; next to water, people may look at fish, lotus flowers, the reflections of the sun and the moon, cultural activities like dragon-boat races, waterside buildings such as pagodas and sculptures as well as natural scenes like the tides or waterfalls. Many waterside pavilions of different functions, layouts, and forms have been built.

Waterside pavilions are not necessarily very close to the water. Some waterside pavilions stand far away from water. The West Lake Scenery Under Heaven Pavilion at Gushan in Hangzhou, for example, is built in a valley, six meters lower than the surrounding terrace. The pond is small, but the pavilion is large. If the pavilion is too close to the bank of the pond, it looks out of proportion. If the pavilion is built some distance away from the pond, not only is the defect avoided, but also the space is broadened, so that visitors inside and outside have a larger space. Most interestingly, the pavilion has a unique couplet on it:

Shuishui shanshan, chuchu mingming xiuxiu;
Water and mountain, everything is bright and elegant;

II-2-5 A close-up view of the West Lake Scenery Under Heaven Pavilion

Qingqing yuyu, shishi haohao qiqi.
Rain or shine, it is always good and unique.

This couplet, with its word repetitions, greatly enhances the landscape. It is said that the couplet was written by the scholar and calligrapher Huang Wenzhong in 1932 (II-2-5).

Most water pavilions are close to water, even touching it. Some are even built on piers or mounds in the water. It is easier for people to enjoy lotus flowers and fish in the ponds from these pavilions. Sometimes water pavilions have inverted reflections in the water (II-2-6 to 9).

II-2-6a A double-eave polygon pavilion in Taoranting Park, Beijing. The pavilion and the green willows complement each other.

II-2-6b The double-eave square pavilion
under the shade of willows in Beijing

II-2-6c The double-eave square pavilion on the banks of West Lake in Hangzhou

II-2-6d A fan-shaped pavilion in the Humble Administrator's Garden, a famous garden south of the Yangtze River

II-2-7a The Fan-shaped Pavilion for Enjoying Lotus Flowers (Beijing)

II-2-7b The Fan-shaped Pavilion for Enjoying Lotus Flowers (Beijing)

II-2-8 A waterside pavilion's
reflection in the water (Jinan)

II-2-9a The Water Corridor Pavilion in a garden in Suzhou

II-2-9b A lake pavilion at the Lingering Garden in Suzhou

II-2-9c A lake pavilion on a man-made platform at the Lingering Garden in Suzhou

II-2-10a A stream pavilion, a resting pavilion by a stream (Shanghai)

II-2-10b A stream pavilion, a resting pavilion by a stream (Changshu)

Some pavilions are built across a stream; they are called stream pavilions. From this kind of pavilion, people can enjoy the sound of running water (II-2-10a,b).

Other pavilions are built in the shape of boats and are called "land boats" or "untied boats." This is a unique element of pavilion design in Chinese gardens (II-2-11).

A particularly interesting fixture is a large mirror in waterside pavilions to bring the water into the pavilion and thus broaden the space. There is such a pavilion in Wangshi Garden in Suzhou. With corridors on both sides, this hexagonal pavilion with a tapered roof is built on a mound of rocks in the water and has a large mirror in it. At night, the bright moon in the sky is reflected in both the water and the mirror. It creates an interesting image of three moons--the moon in the sky, the moon in the water, and the moon in the pavilion. This pavilion is called "The Moon Arrives and Wind Comes." From it we can see how cleverly garden builders have created scenes with pavilions in China (II-2-12).

II-2-11 The "land boat" pavilion (also known as the "untied boat" pavilion) in Guangzhou—the Touching Green Pavilion

II-2-12 A waterside pavilion with a large mirror inside to bring the water into the pavilion and thus broaden the space.

Many pavilions are built in a body of water, accessible by bridge(II-2-13a,b). Those with short bridges are close to the bank and surrounded by water on at least three sides, while long bridges reach the middle of a pond or a lake, where one can have a wide view of the water. The bridges can be flat, arched, or have flights. Visitors walk up and down, to and fro while enjoying the water scene from the bridge (II-2-14a,b). Chuitai in Yangzhou, for example, is a square pavilion on an islet with a long bridge stretching through the lake (Slim West Lake). The pavilion has round doors on three sides. From the doors of the pavilion, one has a clear view of the Five Pavilions Bridge and the White Pagoda. With the White Pagoda towering in the middle, one experiences a beautiful scene (II-2-15).

Mid-lake pavilions have no bridges leading to them; they can be reached only by boat. Generally, small bodies of water do not have mid-lake pavilions. The garden of Prince Gong's Residence in Beijing is an exception. A pavilion stands in the middle of a pond, but the view is not particularly beautiful (II-2-16).

The mid-lake pavilion in West Lake in Hangzhou lies on an islet in the vast stretch of water (560 hectares). Although it is not distinctive in structure or shape, it has

II-2-13a A square pavilion with steps to the bank

II-2-13b A water pavilion with a curved bridge to the bank

II-2-14a A pavilion with a white top and railings. With the inverted reflection in the water, the pavilion looks like a two-story pavilion.

a surrounding wall and round doors on four sides and produces an unique scenic effect: "One pavilion embodies all manifestations of nature; / No dust lies on the four sides" and "Heat disperses with the waves; / A breeze comes from the surface of water." It is a true mid-lake pavilion, with "An endless view on four sides, / It changes with the four seasons." This mid-lake pavilion is a typical example of a water pavilion.

II-2-14b A water pavilion surrounded by trees

II-2-15 View of Chuitai Pavilion on Slim West Lake in Yangzhou through a window

II-2-16 The Mid-lake Pavilion in Prince Gong's Residence in Beijing

II-2-17a A cherry blossom "flower pavilion"

(3) Plant Pavilions (or Flower Pavilions)

Most pavilions have plants (trees and flowers) growing around them for decoration. As mentioned before, some pavilions are hidden in the forest, some are built next to ponds of lotus flowers, and some are surrounded by large stretches of plants and flowers. These are flower pavilions. Many pavilions are named after plants or flowers, such as peony pavilion, plum pavilion, Chinese flowering crabapple pavilion, chrysanthemum pavilion, or bamboo pavilion (II-2-17a,b,c). In Zhongshan Park in Beijing, there is a pavilion next to a pine tree and a cypress tree, so the pavilion is called "Green Pine and Cypress Pavilion(II-2-18)." Flower pavilions inspire many poets and painters, and they produce many works with that motif. The Song Dynasty poet Yang Wanli, for example, wrote many poems about flowers, two of which show how much he enjoyed pavilions and flowers:

Lotus Pavilion
The pavilion stands by the waterside like a little boat;
At night rain came in torrents, beating the seedpods.
The lotus leaves in the morning were completely dry;
I mistake the rain for a gale of evening wind.

II-2-17b A bamboo pavilion

II-2-17c A chrysanthemum pavilion containing a statue of Tao Yuanming (376 - 427), a famous poet who loved chrysanthemums.

The poet compares the pavilion by a large lotus pond to a little boat. At night he hears the sound of rain beating the lotus seedpods, but how did he know that he had mistaken when he thought he heard a wind? He realized that lotus leaves do not get wet in the rain.

Pond Pavilion and Two Plum Trees
The blooming plum blossoms are half withered,
Two branches laden with bright snow stand in the cold.
Clustered golden shower trees are hidden from sight,
The best view is from the pavilion over the pond.

The poet compares the purely white plum blossoms with snow on a bright day and thinks that the best view can be had only by gazing from the pavilion over the stretch of water.

The emotion of enjoying flowers in pavilions is very subtle. The Song Dynasty woman poet Li Qingzhao describes in her "Stream Pavilion at Sunset": "Losing myself fully in pleasure, I return my boat late, / I went deep into the lotus flowers by mistake." The poet enjoys lotus flowers while rowing a boat. As illustrated (II-2-19), the lotus pond may be small, but the emotion of "rowing a boat in the depth of lotus flowers" is profound.

II-2-19 A pavilion in a lotus pond where one can row a boat

II-2-21a Flower pavilion

Some pavilions are built in the shape of flowers. The pavilion pictured (II-2-20) is in the shape of a five-petal plum blossom. Although it is on a small path and lack architectural depth, the idea is original.

The pavilions in the pictures (II-2-21a,b,c) demonstrate the environmental value of the pavilion building art. One is a "Flower Pavilion" with a roof made of flowers like morning glory, the other is a "Colorful Grass Pavilion" covered entirely by green or red grass, the third is a "Cypress Pavilion" with a five-pointed, tapered roof made by growing five pine and cypress trees together. All this demonstrates the exquisite art of Chinese gardening.

II-2-21b A square grass pavilion

II-2-20 A plum blossom-shaped pavilion

3. Pavilions for Cultural Activities

Chinese culture's 5,000-year history is greatly reflected in pavilions.

For instance, the dragon was the symbol of the emperor. It was a mythical animal representing one of the twelve zodiac signs of the year in which a person is born. Gradually it became the symbol of China herself, including her culture and people. As such, dragon pavilions have emerged in many places, such as religious temples and gardens. The Dragon Pavilion of Kaifeng, Henan Province, mentioned earlier, is also a palace symbolizing the emperor's majesty. To commemorate the year 1987, the Year of the Dragon in the zodiac, a dragon pavilion was built in Dragon Pool Park in Beijing whose corridor winds its way like a dragon, markedly different than other square or round pavilions (II-3-1a,b).

From the Han Dynasty (206 B.C.— A.D.220) to the Wei and Jin dynasties, a custom gradually developed on the third day of the third lunar month. On that day, people bathed in lakes to wash away unluckiness, after which they would drink wine and write poems by the running water. Eventually, special pavilions of "meandering water and floating cups" were substituted for bodies of water. These pavilions contained twisting, long, slightly inclined grooves in the floor filled with water. People sat

II-3-1b The entrance to the Dragon Pavilion of the Dragon Pool Park in Beijing

II-3-2a The Imperial Tablet Pavilion at Lanting in Shaoxing

beside the grooves and put cups in them. The cup floated down the groove, and when it stopped in front of someone, that person was required to drink and write a poem.

The Pavilion of Floating Cups, near a stream at Lanting, Shaoxing in Zhejiang Province, probably is the oldest of its kind in Chinese history. On the third day of the third lunar month of the ninth year of the reign of the Yonghe Emperor (A.D.353) during the Jin Dynasty, Wang Xizhi (307–365) a calligrapher and Officer of the Right Army, invited 42 scholars to enjoy an afternoon of "floating cups." Later, he collected all the poems the scholars wrote during their games into an album, himself writing the famous "Preface to the Orchid Pavilion Collection."

Today, Lanting has become famous for its calligraphy. Little Lanting was built during the reign of the Emperor Jiajing of the Ming Dynasty (1368–1644) with a goose pond in front and a small triangle pavilion at the side. In the pavilion there was a stone tablet inscribed with Goose Pond, written by the father and son team of Wang Xizhi (307–365) and Wang Xianzhi (344–386). A stream winds its way at the back of the pond and by the stream is the Pavilion of Floating Cups. Behind that pavilion is the Imperial Tablet Pavilion, with the height of 12.5 m. A stone

tablet is set up in it, inscribed on the front with the "Preface to the Orchid Pavilion Collection" in the calligraphy of Emperor Kangxi (1654–1722) and "Poem for Orchid Pavilion" on the back by Emperor Qianlong (1711–1799). To the east of this scenic spot, Ink Pavilion stands above a pond named "Ink Pond," whose walls are embedded with ten kinds of stone tablets with inscriptions of "Preface to the Orchid Pavilion Collection" copied by calligraphers from as far back as the Tang Dynasty (618–907). (II-3-2a,b)

Floating cup pavilions can still be seen in many places, such as Yigan Pavilion (II-3-3a,b) in the Tanzhe Temple,

II-3-3a A panoramic view of the Pavilion of Floating Cups (Yigan Pavilion) in the Tanzhe Temple in Beijing .

II-3-2b The Little Orchid Pavilion at Lanting in Shaoxing

Liushuiyin Pavilion in Zhongnanhai, Xishang Pavilion in Emperor Qianlong's Garden in the Forbidden City, Qinqiu Pavilion in the mansion of Imperial Prince Gong, all of them in Beijing, and the Pavilion of Floating Cup in Wenjin Chamber in the Summer Resort of Chengde in Hebei Province.

Another means by which pavilions reflect Chinese culture is through stories. For example, a beautiful Tang Dynasty love story, *The Dragon King's Daughter,* has been a popular opera for generations. The hero of the story, Liu Yi, risked his life to go to the Dragon King's palace to write a story for the dragon king's daughter. Today a "Liu Yi Well" is still well preserved, next to the

II-3-3b The meandering "river" on the floor of the Pavilion of Floating Cups in the Tanzhe Temple in Beijing

II-3-4 The Pavilion of the Dragon King's Daughter on Mount Jun in Yueyang

II-3-5a A panoramic view of Lixia Pavilion on Daming Lake, Jinan

II-3-5b The couplets on Lixia Pavilion on Daming Lake, Jinan

Dongting Lake in Yueyang City, Hunan Province. Above the well was a double pavilion named Chuanshu Pavilion (II-3-4). It is said to be the place where Liu Yi went down to the Dragon palace through the Dongting Lake. The water of the ever-flowing well is so clean and sweet that it can be used to make excellent tea and wine. This pavilion became a scenic spot combining the spring, the pavilion, and the legend.

Drinking and writing poems in pavilions were very popular in ancient times. Lixia Pavilion on Daming Lake in Jinan, Shandong Province is one example. In 745, Du Fu (712 – 770), a famous Tang Dynasty poet once invited Li Yong (a famous calligrapher) to drink in the pavilion. Du Fu wrote a poem that included the line: "Old is this pavilion in Haiyou; / Many are the literati in Jinan," which became the couplet on the pillars of the pavilion (II-3-5a,b).

Canglang Pavilion is one of the oldest pavilions in private gardens in Suzhou. It was built on a small hill when Su Dongpo (1037–1101), a famous writer and calligrapher of the Northern Song Dynasty, was demoted to a low position in Suzhou. The name of the pavilion (II-3-7), meaning "gentle waves," was given because Su Dongpo wanted to retire from public life there. Su often

II-3-6a A panoramic view of the Crane-Releasing Pavilion on Mount Gu in Hangzhou

II-3-6b Interior of the Crane-Releasing Pavilion on Mount Gu in Hangzhou

drank in the pavilion with his friends Ouyang Xiu (1007–1072, a historian) and Mei Yaochen (1002–1060, a poet) and others.

Lin Bu (967 – 1029), a famous hermit, withdrew from society and lived in solitude on an isolated mountaintop in Hangzhou, calling the plums his wife and the cranes his sons. Every day he practiced the zither, played chess, read books, painted pictures, enjoyed nature, and wrote many excellent poems. He was greatly admired by the people. Later, the people built the Crane-Releasing Pavilion (II-3-6a,b) as a memorial to him.

The Academy of Mount Yuelu, in Changsha, Hunan Province, has a history of 2,000 years. Zhu Xi (1130–1200) and Zhang Shi (1133–1180), both Confucian philosophers taught there. The academy contains Hexitai Pavilion, built on a raised terrace with a gabled roof and two walls on the side (II-3-8). In the pavilion there is a stone tablet inscribed with the poems of Zhu Xi, Zhang Shi, Wang Shouren (1472 – 1529, a philosopher), and Chairman Mao Zedong (1893 – 1976). The roof beam has inscriptions of Chairman Mao's poems. The other things that attract the eyes are the two huge Chinese characters, "Blessing" and "Longevity."

In Yongjia, Zhejiang Province, there is a small village

II-3-7 Canglang Pavilion
in Suzhou

清風明月本無價

II-3-8 A panoramic view of Hexitai Pavilion in the
Academy of Mount Yuelu in Changsha

with many ponds. In the Ming Dynasty (1368 - 1644) many pavilions were built on the ponds. The one that is still extant today is a double-eave pavilion in the style of the Ming Dynasty (II-3-9).

Zhongshan Park in Beijing was originally an altar to the god of the land and grain built in the Ming Dynasty. In 1914 it was turned into a public park after the Xinhai democratic revolution led by Dr Sun Yat-sen overthrew the Qing Dynasty. The park contains several distinctive pavilions, such as Xili Pavilion, which was a pavilion in Honglu Temple built for foreign guests to rehearse for meetings with the emperor. It was moved to Zhongshan Park in 1917. Used in both the Ming and Qing dynasties, it is the oldest and best-preserved hexagonal pavilion with a square roof (II-3-10).

Actually, playing music and drinking in pavilions was first popularized in the Tang Dynasty. One example of a "Pavilion for Playing Music" was recorded in the preface to "Poem Written on a Pond" by Bai Juyi (772 - 846), a Tang Dynasty poet. Another is in Guiyuan Temple in Wuchang, which still contains a stone tablet inscribed with Musical Terrace. Clearly, playing music in pavilions is an ancient tradition. Contemporary examples include a bamboo garden at Huanglong Cave in Hangzhou,

II-3-10 A side view of Xili Pavilion in Zhongshan Park, Beijing

where there is a small triangular pavilion in which girls wearing ancient costumes play music for tourists (II-3-11a). At the octagonal Pavilion of Fragrant Snow (II-3-11b), Shaoxing opera performances are put on for tourists. Those entertainments enrich both people's lives and the pavilion culture.

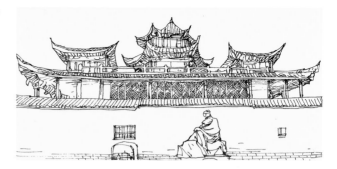

II-4-1 Ziyun Pavilion of Western Shu in Mianyang, Sichuan Province

4. Memorial Pavilions

Many pavilions are built to commemorate people or items of political, cultural, sociological, or moral significance. Those pavilions, far from being isolated, are grouped with statues, stone tablets, cultural relics, small buildings and even trees to form a "pavilion park." For example, East Lake Park in Fengxiang, Shaanxi Province has the largest number of pavilions, almost 30. The Park of a Hundred Pavilions in Taoranting Park, Beijing, has memorial pavilions commemorating famous persons of almost every dynasty. We will go into greater depth on this topic in the next chapter.

Often, ancient pavilions have been renovated and repaired many times. For example, Ziyun Pavilion of Western Shu, on Western Mountain in Mianyang, Sichuan Province was first built in the Sui Dynasty (589—618) and has been rebuilt each dynasty since.

The poet Liu Yuxi (772—842) wrote the line, "Zhuge Cottage of Southern Yang, Ziyun Pavilion of Western Shu" in "On My Modest Room" about Yang Xiong (53 B.C.—A.D.18), a famous thinker and writer of the Western Han Dynasty (206 B.C—A.D.22). A memorial pavilion was built to commemorate him, and the writer Guo Moruo (1892—1978) wrote an inscription on the horizontal plaque of the pavilion. In 1987, the extended memorial pavilion,

Yunü Spring, the place where Yang Xiong studied,General Jiang Wan's tomb,the Ancestral Temple of Marquis for Revering the Sage, Western Mountain Taoist Temple were combined into a cultural park.

There is a story about Fangfan Pavilion in Haifeng, Guangdong Province. In 1278, Zhang Hongfan, a Song general who had surrendered to the Mongol troops, launched a surprise attack on Wen Tianxiang and his army who were preparing dinner on the Wuling slope in Haifeng. Wen Tianxiang and his army lost the battle. Wen was captured and killed by the Mongols. People built the pavilion in 1506 to commemorate him. The pavilion looks simple and unsophisticated, with red bricks and green tiles. A stone tablet has engraved on it the story of the battle of Wuling slope, including the couplet: "In my hot blood there is only Song; / In the mountains of my loyalty, how can there be anyone else?"

The new Ziyun Pavilion of Western Shu was built to augment the fame of the city of Mianyang, with a history of more than 2,100 years (II-4-1). However, the size and style of the newly built one do not match the original

Ziyun Pavilion of Western Shu described in "On My Modest Room." The new pavilion is a five-story building 23 meters high with 128 pillars. Plus the accompanying pavilions and mansions, the complex occupies an area of 1,400 square meters. Moreover, the new one does not accord with the story and the person being commemorated.

Qiufeng Pavilion, facing the Yangtze River, stands on the mountainside of the Jinzi Mountain of Badong in the area of the Three Gorges of Yangtze River. Trees thrive around it. It is a memorial pavilion for Song Prime Minister Kou Zhun (961–1023). It is a square pavilion with eight pillars and double turned up eaves.

The Pavilion of Lord Fan, originally named Li Spring Pavilion, stands in the Ancestral Temple of Lord Fan, commemorating Vice Palace Secretary Fan Zhongyan (989–1052), who was framed by other officials and demoted to a low position in Qingzhou (present-day Yidu in Shandong Province). The local people deeply respected him because of his integrity and changed the original name into Pavilion of Lord Fan. In the pavilion there is a covered spring and three ancient trees. In the back yard of Ancestral Temple of Lord Fan we can find another pavilion called Houle Pavilion, named for a fa-

mous line in Fan Zhongyan's "On Yueyang Tower": "Be the first to worry about the affairs of the state, but the last to enjoy oneself."

Wind and Rain Pavilion was built in 1953 to the west of Xiling Bridge on West Lake in Hangzhou. It commemorates Qiu Jin (1875–1907), a revolutionary patriotic heroine (II-4-2). The name was taken from a line in the last poem she wrote before her death: "wind and rain in autumn, pain of heart." The pavilion has an inclined square roof and weeping willows around it. To the east of Xiling Bridge there stands a statue of Qiu Jin, wearing long skirt with a sword in her hand and her head raised like a knight. Away from the pavilion, the statue looks lonely.

In the Qinghua University there are many memorial pavilions commemorating famous historical figures.

Ziqing Pavilion

Lying on the east bank of the pond which is to the north of the building "Shuimu Qinghua" in Qinghua University, it was originally an ancient pavilion named Yidong. In 1978, on the 30th anniversary of Zhu Ziqing's death (1898–1948), it was renamed Ziqing Pavilion (II-4-3). Zhu Ziqing, also known as Pei Xuan, was born in Donghai, Jiangsu Province and was a famous scholar

II-4-2 The Wind and Rain Pavilion, to the west of Xiling Bridge in Hangzhou

II-4-3 Ziqing Pavilion in Qinghua University

II-4-4 A panoramic view of Wen Pavilion in Qinghua University

who taught Chinese literature in Qinghua University. There is a white statue of Zhu Ziqing on the north bank of the pond.

Wen Pavilion

Wen Pavilion (II-4-4) is located on a small hill to the west of the auditorium in Qinghua University. On the path leading to the pavilion is a stone tablet with an inscription: "This is an ancient pavilion; after the victory of the War of Resistance Against Japanese Aggression it was renamed Wen Pavilion as a memorial to Wen Yiduo (1899 −1946)."

Wen Yiduo was born in Xishui, Hubei Province. He was a famous scholar, poet, a fighter for democracy, and professor of Chinese at Qinghua University. He participated in the May 4th Movement of 1919 (an anti-imperialist, anti-feudal political and cultural movement influenced by the Russian Revolution and Communism and led by intellectuals).

On the top of the small hill, a black marble stone tablet and statue of Wen Yiduo have been built.

Han Pavilion

On the southeast bank of the historic Jinchun Park in Qinghua University are a series of pavilions connected

with corridors (II-4-5). They were constructed to commemorate Wu Han (1909 – 1969), the famous historian and Qinghua University professor. The name of the pavilion is in the handwriting of Deng Xiaoping. To the north of the pavilions is a statue of Wu Han.

Guibao Pavilion (II-4-6)

Guibao Pavilion was built as a memorial to commemorate the 100th anniversary of the birth of Song Qingling (1893 – 1981), wife of Sun Yat-sen and vice-chairwoman of the People's Republic of China. The pavilion was named Guibao (or Jewel) because Premier Zhou Enlai once honored her as "the jewel of China". It has a double-eave round roof and five pillars decorated with plum blossoms, symbolizing Song Qingling's nobility.

Some pavilions are erected not to commemorate people but things — such as ancient trees — or events of special significance.

For example, a tablet pavilion can be found in Hongtong, Shanxi Province. In the pavilion stands a stone tablet with inscription, "The Place for Ancient Trees," with an ancient wall nearby. On the wall hangs a banner inscribed, "Colonial Relics" (II-4-7).

In Yue Temple, Hangzhou, there is a Jingzhongbai Pavilion, with eight fossils of an ancient cypress. It is said that the cypress withered away after Yue Fei (1103 −1142), a patriotic general of the Southern Song Dynasty was framed and died. The cypress supposedly can cure diseases. (II-4-8)

II-4-7 The Memorial Pavilion of Ancient Trees at Hongtong County, Shanxi Province

II-4-8 Jingzhongbai Pavilion in Yue Temple, Hangzhou

5. Pavilions for Protection

Pavilions are built to shelter tablet inscriptions, famous stones, wells and springs, or statues that would suffer damage by rain, wind, and pollution if in the open air. Most tablets are of cultural and commemorative significance, and thus the major function of pavilions is protection. Lookout pavilions on city walls and common sentry boxes for sentries have protective functions, and gate pavilions play both a protective and symbolic role. All the above-mentioned pavilions can be classified into the category of pavilions for protection.

Pavilions housing stone tablets are the most common protective pavilions in China's scenic gardens. Most such pavilions have the tablet freestanding in the center of the pavilion, some have the tablet inlaid in the wall of the pavilion, and a few have the tablet standing beside the pavilion. The principal part of a pavilion housing a tablet is the tablet, and based on the tablet's contents, such pavilions may be categorized as follows:

(1) Pavilions Housing a Tablet Inscribed with the Name of the Scene

These tablets signify scenic spots. Take the ten famous views of West Lake in Hangzhou as an example.

At each scenic spot, there is a pavilion housing a tablet with the scene s name, such as Listening to Orioles by the Waving Willows, Autumn Moon in the Smooth Lake, and Watching Fish at Huagang. Some tablets bear only the place name. For instance, at Dayu's Mausoleum located in Shaoxing, Zhejiang Province, there is a pavilion housing a tablet with only the three Chinese characters of "Dayu Mausoleum." On the back of most tablets with names of scenes are poems or essays praising the scenery (II-5-1a,b) (II-5-2).

(2) Memorial Pavilions

Memorial pavilions are discussed in other sections. However, it is worth stating that in recent years, each province has made donations to renovate the Great Wall and thereafter put up pavilions and tablets for commemoration.

For example, the Guizhou Pavilion Housing A Tablet at the Badaling Great Wall is typical of Guizhou design. The four pillars of the pavilion are covered with red granite, on which rest two crossbeams covered with grayish-white granite; two big plates on the roof of the pavil-

II-5-1b *The Pavilion of the Autumn Moon in the Smooth Lake*

II-5-2 *The Pavilion of the Moon Over Reed Gully at Dawn, Beijing*

II-5-3 The Imperial Tablet Pavilion at the Buddhist Felicity and Longevity Temple in Chengde

ion are placed crisscross on the beams. This unique design, resembling the temporary work sheds built by the "Guizhou Camp" builders when constructing the Great Wall, is inelegant but stable. It complements the tremendous momentum of the Great Wall. In the pavilion, there stands a tablet made of black jade and marble with an eight-character inscription: "Love our Chinese nation, repair our Great Wall." The rear and side faces of the tablet are carved with depictions of the patriotism of the people of Guizhou in their contributions to renovate the Great Wall. Beside the pavilion is a distinctive oval-shaped bench.

(3) Imperial Pavilions Housing a Tablet

These pavilions are left by emperors while sightseeing, particularly Emperor Qianlong of the Qing Dynasty. Qianlong toured the regions south of the Yangtze River six times, and each time he visited a new place, he wrote poems and calligraphy, which were then inscribed on tablets to commemorate the occasion. Pavilions were put up over the tablets for protection, and hence the imperial pavilion housing a tablet became a relatively common yet distinctive type of pavilion in scenic gardens. Such pavilions usually have a thick, heavy, and stately

II-5-4a The Pavilion of the Holy Floodgate Pool houses a stone tablet at the bank of the West Lake in Hangzhou. The tablet, inscribed "On Qiantang Stone Lake," is embedded in the outside wall of the pavilion. The pavilion contains the switch of the floodgate of West Lake.

appearance; many are quite large. They are always reddish brown with a double-eave, glazed roof, and they bear the lofty quality of imperial dignity, especially those in temples, palaces, and mausoleums. The tablet itself is handsomely built. The top is usually carved with a dragon pattern, and in all cases, the tablet is set on a terrapin podium, signifying longevity and health to the ordained Son of Heaven (namely, the emperor). For example, the imperial tablet at the Buddhist Felicity and Longevity Temple in Chengde is made of an eight-meter-high megalith and is carved with an inscription by Emperor Qianlong (II-5-3).

In short, pavilions housing a tablet are generally carved with essays, poems, paintings, or sculptures. They are historic and cultural works of art combining carving, poetry, and painting; they are an important part of the Chinese literary and artistic treasury. Since the inscriptions on the tablets are different, the pavilions erected to protect them are also different in connotation and appearance (II-5-4a,b,c).

II-5-4c The Crane-Releasing Pavilion, a thatched-roof pavilion housing a stone tablet built by villagers.

*II-5-5a The Stone-Protecting
Pavilion in a garden of Suzhou*

Stone–Protecting Pavilions

A beautiful stone can either be unique in shape or re-semble a scene. It may be beautiful in luster: white like jade, yellow like wax, or a riot of colors. It may be beau-tiful in texture, with a clear grain, creating different im-pressions viewed from near or far. Such stones are con-sidered treasures and often are protected by pavilions (II-5-5a). Some are natural, with engraved characters on them describing the scenery. Picture II-5-5b shows the Secluded Streamlet Pavilion in Gaoming Temple on Mount Tiantai in Zhejiang Province, whose name came from the scene name "Secluded Streamlet" carved on a natural stone. A pavilion was put up over the stone to protect it, and a pavilion couplet, was written describing the scene inside and outside the pavilion in two sentences. The couplet is as follows:

A pavilion completely holds the moon beside the plum trees;
A secluded path is added to fresh wind from beyond the bamboo.

Here, the pavilion plays a significant role in enhancing the scenes.

*II-5-5b The Secluded Streamlet Pavilion
on Mount Tiantai, Zhejiang Province*

Other stones became famous because of beautiful and romantic stories associated with them, and thus pavilions were put up to protect them. For example, the Tingsong Pavilion (the Pavilion for Listening to Pines) on Mount Hui in Wuxi has a large brown stone in the center with a smooth surface for sitting or lying on. This stone is called the "Stone to Lie On" or "Stone Bed." One side of the "bed" is carved with inscriptions left by scholars in the Song Dynasty. On the south side are two worn, hardly-recognizable Chinese seal characters, "Listening to Pines," written by Tang Dynasty calligrapher Li Yangbing. The stone bed was originally placed in front of the Hall of Sakyamuni in Huishan Temple. In the Ming Dynasty during the reign of Emperor Zhengde (1506-1522), the county magistrate moved it to its current position under a gingko tree, and a pavilion was built to protect it. The pavilion is hexagonal; its one side is a wall with a horizontal board bearing the pavilion's name; in the center of the wall is a glass-encased black stone tablet inscribed with the "Record of Listening to the Wind in the Pines on the Stone Bed." On the upper right corner of the tablet hangs a small board which tells of the history of the stone bed. It is said that when King Kang of the Song Dynasty, also called Zhao Gou, fled south from Jingdu to Hangzhou, he passed Mount Hui, where he saw this stone and used it as a bed. At midnight, he suddenly heard the sound of the wind in the pines, and, thinking that the Jin soldiers were chasing him, he immediately arose and ran. People of later generations named the stone the Tingsong Stone, or Stone for Listening to Pines.

In modern times, the famous musician Hua Yanjun (A Bing), composed a music named "Ting Song" (Listening to Pines), characterized by its cheerful patriotism.

Pavilions Housing a Well

Pavilions housing wells were very common in the past. It not only protected sources of fresh water, but also usually added to natural scenes and complemented man-made landscapes.

In the countryside or areas that are far from rivers and lakes, people rely on wells to obtain their drinking water. Rough thatched sheds or stone pavilions (II-5-6a) protect most wells near houses, roads, and fields.

*II-5-6a The Stone Well Pavilion at
Huilongtan in Shanghai*

In cities, among well-preserved well pavilions, the ones in the Palace Museum, Beijing come first. This Imperial Palace is a huge complex of thousands of rooms. Although the emperor's personal drinking water came from Mount Yuquan, all the household water in the Palace came from wells. According to statistics, there are nearly 100 wells in the Imperial Palace, almost one or two in each courtyard. Most of these wells are protected by pavilions. Two special examples are the four-pillar, octagonal pavilions standing outside the Tianyi Gate of the Imperial Garden, which are of novel structure and exquisite appearance. Each of the two pavilions occupies a small area, about three square meters, and they have a low but exquisitely engraved "Lute Balustrade." The roof is open to the sky above the mouth of the well; this is either for light or an imitation of ancient practices. (II-5-6b,c).

Why open a hole on the roof of pavilions housing a well? The answer lies in a superstition of feudal society. According to palace tradition, if water is not exposed to sunlight, it becomes unhealthful and people who drink it will fall ill. Therefore, the roof of the pavilion is open to let in natural light for the water. Although this practice has no scientific basis, an open roof does allow people to

*II-5-6b A panoramic view of the well
pavilion in the Imperial Garden of the
Imperial Palace in Beijing*

II-5-6c Interior of the well pavilion in the Imperial Garden of the Imperial Palace in Beijing. The well is now covered by a round stone table.

see the quality and quantity of the well's water more clearly.

Another type of pavilion is the pavilion over a spring, which protects water, especially famous springs from stories, legends, and anecdotes.

For example, there is a Liuyi Spring Pavilion (II-5-7) in Hangzhou built at the foot of a small hill beside a stream. Legend has it that the famous Song Dynasty writer Su Dongpo (1037-1101) had the pavilion built during

II-5-7 Liuyi Spring Pavilion in Hangzhou

II-5-8 The Pavilion of the Ancient Well for Transporting Wood at Jingci Temple, Hangzhou

his term as a government official in Hangzhou, in memory of his good friend Ouyang Xiu.

There is a hexagonal pavilion with tapered roof in Jingci Temple, Hangzhou which houses a dry well. In the bottom of the well is a piece of wood with the following legend: Monk Jigong was transporting wood from Sichuan through this well to build the temple. He was removing the wood from the well when finally, a voice said, "Enough." There was still one piece of wood in the well, and it remains there to this day. Hence the well was once called "Well for Gods' Transportation" and now is called the "Ancient Well for Transporting Wood" (II-5-8).

The ancient Jin Ancestral Temple has a history of more than 1,500 years. It has a spring called "Nanlao Spring" (Won't Age Spring), one of the three matchless treasures of Jin Ancestral Temple. It is said that the spring is the source of the Jin River in Shanxi Province. The water gushes from the ground with a normal temperature of 17 degrees Celsius; the spring has been gushing water for 1,000 years without stopping throughout the year. Its color is like jade, and it provided irrigation for thousands of acres of fine land. It was named Won't Age Spring after a line from the Lu Section of the ancient *Book of Songs*: "Won't age for thousands of years." (II-5-9)

Over the pond fed by Nanlao Spring is a pavilion named "Untied Boat." The pavilion is small and the pond is even smaller, a rare characteristic of spring pavilions.

The Tang Dynasty "Tea Master" Lu Yu selected the name of the Pavilion of the Second Spring Under Heaven in Xihui Park, Wuxi (II-5-10). Pavilions typically protect such famous springs . The pavilion unifies the view and acts as a focal point. The blind musician Hua Yanjun composed a famous piece, "The Moon Mirrored in Two Springs," making the spring well known all over China.

II-5-9 A panoramic view of the Nanlao Spring
Pavilion at the Jin Ancestral Temple, Taiyuan

II-5-10 The Pavilion of the Second
Spring Under Heaven in Wuxi

II-5-11 *The door pavilion at the entrance to the Dragon Pavilion in Kaifeng*

Door Pavilions

Door pavilions in scenic gardens mainly have a protective function. They also play a representative and symbolic role as the gateway to scenic spots. Thus, the pavilions must have a relatively high artistic value and complement the features of the scenic spot.

For example, Dragon Pavilion in Kaifeng was originally a Song Dynasty palace, and therefore its door pavilion has a glazed roof with a side-hall in the same style. The plaque is inscribed with the two Chinese characters "Song Hu" (Cry out on Mount Song), linking the pavilion with the famous Mountain. All this reflects the greatness of royalty. (II-5-11)

The door pavilions of the gates of the famous Taoist area of Qingcheng Mountain, are both covered with black tile, a natural and simple design coordinating with the religious aura of the mountain (II-5-12).

The door pavilion at the mouth of Qixia Cave, one of Hangzhou's scenic spots, has one side open for passage and a round window in the opposite wall for selling tickets and goods. The pavilion has protruding points and whitewashed walls that preserve the natural simplicity of architecture in regions south of the Yangtze River (II-5-13).

II-5-12 *The door pavilion on the second peak of Mount Qingcheng in Chengdu*

II-5-13 The door pavilion at Qixia Cave in Hangzhou

II-5-14a The door pavilion at the Lotus Root Garden in Suzhou

II-5-14b The entrance to "the garden within a garden" in Wuxi

The door pavilion at the south gate of Taoranting Park in Beijing, is a hexagonal double-pavilion with protruding points. It integrates with other small corridors in a group, not only giving prominence to the pavilion, but also meeting the needs of the entrance of a park

Other gate pavilions of private gardens south of the Yangtze River adopt diverse shapes, either a pavilion at the gate or inside the house as a separation device, and different styles – either relatively simple just for passage, or very elaborate as a gateway leading to scenery (II-5-14a,b,c).

II-5-14c The gate of the "detached garden" in Suzhou

Moreover, another typical protective pavilion is the lookout pavilion. Picture II-5-15 shows one — a place for policemen to control traffic, entrance guards to watch a gate, or patrolmen to make their rounds. It is quite simple and practical. By contrast, the lookout corner towers on the wall of the Palace Museum, built in the Ming and Qing dynasties, are elaborately designed in an imposing royal manner. Although they follow the style of pavilions, they do not fall into the category of pavilions in scenic gardens, and therefore are not included in this book.

II-6-1a The bell pavilion at the Six-Harmony Pagoda in Hangzhou

6. Religious Pavilions

Pavilions are built in monasteries and temples for various religious activities. For instance, monks' daily routine includes tolling a bell in the morning and beating a drum at dusk, so the main hall of a temple is usually flanked by Bell Pavilion and Drum Pavilion (II-6-1a,b), in addition to special pavilions built to protect Buddhist statues, pagodas, tombs, and memorial tablets of gods (II-6-2a,b). Other religious pavilions include pavilions for burning joss sticks or offering donations and Pavilion of Merit and Virtue (II-6-3). The imperial temple or altar includes an Animal Pavilion where animals were slaughtered as sacrificial offerings (II-6-4). In addition there are many kinds of pavilions for the bodies of dead monks. In Taoist temples, visitors can find special pavilions for making pills of immortality. All these pavilions have important religious functions (II-6-5 to II-6-6).

In the Qing Dynasty, during the God-Welcoming Fair, the people of Guangdong Province carried a "deity pavilion" to parade in the street, praying to the gods to drive away evil, subdue demons and maintain peace. Such deity pavilions were very elaborate and exquisite wood sculptures.

II-6-1b An imitation of the drum pavilion at Hancheng, Guangzhou

II-6-2a A panoramic view of the Pavilion of the Buddha Preaching Dharma in a temple

II-6-2b The Temple of the Memorial Tablet of the Deities of Heaven and Earth

II-6-3 The Pavilion of Merit and Virtue

II-6-4 A panoramic view of the Slaughterhouse
Pavilion at the Altar of Earth Park in Beijing

II-6-6 The Collection Pavilion at the Temple
of National Purity on Mount Tiantai

II-6-5 The Pavilion of Lord Guan's
Tomb at Guanlin, Luoyang

II-6-7 The Eight-Diagram Pavilion at Lord Zhou's Temple in Shaanxi

Some temples and shrines in China have nothing to do with religion; they were constructed for people to worship eminent historical figures. For instance, the Lord Zhou Temple was constructed at Fengming Hill, Qishan County, Shaanxi Province to commemorate Lord Zhou (whose name was Jidan), who made great contributions in assisting King Cheng of Zhou of the pre-Qin period to administer the country. Later generations also set up other tablets and statues in many places (II-6-7).

Zhuge Liang was a famous politician and strategist of the state of Shu during the Three Kingdoms period (220 −280). Many of his strategies for using military force and ruling the country have become a part of Chinese culture. To commemorate him, a temple was built at Wuzhangyuan in Qishan County, Shaanxi Province. The overall outlay of Zhuge Liang's Temple is very similar to a religious temple. It includes a Bell Pavilion, Drum Pavilion and a unique Eight-Diagram Pavilion. In Chinese opera, Zhuge Liang traditionally wears an eight-diagram robe and in combating enemies, he created the eight-diagram battle array to confuse invading troops. Hence the people constructed an eight-diagram pavilion in his memory. The pavilion is high and large, with color painted patterns and the design of eight diagrams on the ceiling.

II-6-8 The door pavilion at Zhuge Liang's Temple at Wuzhangyuan, Shaanxi Province

II-6-9 The Apricot Terrace Pavilion in the Temple of Confucius at Qufu, Shandong Province

Unfortunately, the courtyard where the Eight-Diagram Pavilion is located is rather cramped.

In the Temple of Confucius at Qufu, Shandong Province, a square pavilion with double eaves sits on a high terrace where Confucius gave lectures during the Spring and Autumn period (770−476 B.C.). Surrounded by apricot trees, it is also known as Apricot Terrace. It was not until the Jin Dynasty (1115−1234) when a pavilion was built on the terrace. In the Chinese history, pavilions have rarely been used for teachers to give lectures (II-6-9).

The pavilion by the gate of Huanglong Cave in Hangzhou, is in the shape of a Taoist priest's hat, and is about 10 m wide with double eaves. The gatepost couplet reads: "The Yellow Pond will never dry up; and Laozi will always be the best," reflecting the main current of Taoism. The walls of the pavilion are yellow and blue, the representative colors of Taoism (II-6-10).

II-6-10 The door pavilion of the Taoist Temple at Huanglong Cave in Hangzhou

II-7-1a Mother and son pavilions in Shanghai

7. Group Pavilions

Usually pavilions stand alone. Sometimes, they stand next to each other in pairs. If one is large and the other small, they are known as mother and son pavilions; two similar-sized pavilions are called sister pavilions; and two pavilions that are linked together are called twin pavilions (II-7-1a,b,c). If three or more pavilions stand nearby, they are known as group pavilions. Pavilion groups are varied in shapes and layouts. Some are linked to each other as a whole; some are scattered here and there; and others are connected with by bridges and corridors (II-7-2a,b,c).

Dating back to the Tang Dynasty, the poet Bai Juyi wrote an article entitled "Travel Notes on the Five Pavilions," which describes the five pavilions in Baipinzhou to the southeast of Huzhou City. The one spanning a large stream is known as Baipin Pavilion; the one with a profusion of flowers vying for beauty is known as Fragrance Gathering Pavilion; the one where people may enjoy a view of a succession of ever higher green peaks is named Mountain Scenery Pavilion; the one for viewing the sunrise is called Rosy Dawn Pavilion; and the one by the water is named Green Wave Pavilion. In the five pavilions, one may enjoy the most magnificent scenery on earth. Though these five pavilions are

II-7-1b Double-eave twin pavilions in Beijing

II-7-1c Hexagonal twin pavilions in Kunming

II-7-2a Triple pavilions in Taiyuan

II-7-2b The five assembled pavilions arranged in a square in Tianjin

II-7-2c The three pavilions standing in line in Beijing

not a typical pavilion group, they are located near to each other.

Fuzheng Park in Luoyang was a famous garden of the Northern Song Dynasty. In the park is a bamboo grove with five scattered pavilions. They are named Congyu, Pifeng, Yigang, Jiazhu, and Jianshan, respectively. They stand near each other and face one another but are not linked.

Jingshan Hill in Beijing has five peaks, and each peak has a pavilion at the summit. The central peak is the highest, about 43 m high. A square pavilion with double eaves stands on the peak. It is called Wanchun (Ten Thousand Springs) Pavilion, 17.4 m high, with an area of 292.4 sq m. Standing in Wanchun Pavilion, visitors may have a bird's-eye view of the former imperial palace and the city proper of Beijing. The other four pavilions are Guanmiao (Wonderful View) Pavilion and Zhoushang (Surrounding View) Pavilion in the east and Jifang (Harmonious Fragrance) Pavilion and Fulan (Panoramic View) Pavilion in the west. Formerly each of the pavilions contained a bronze statue of a god, the five of which were collectively known as the Five Flavor Gods. Hidden among green trees, the five pavilions do not face each other. With respects to their layout and contents, they should be regarded as a pavilion group (II-7-3).

II-7-3 The Harmonious Fragrance Pavilion, one of the five pavilions on Jingshan Hill in Beijing

II-7-4a A panoramic view of the Five Dragon Pavilions in Beihai Park, Beijing

*II-7-4b The Five Dragon Pavilions
are connected by bridges.*

*II-7-4b The Five Dragon Pavilions
are connected by bridges.*

*II-7-4c The Moisture Fragrance Pavilion,
one of the Five Dragon Pavilions*

On the northwest bank of Beihai Park are the Five Dragon Pavilions, constructed in the Ming Dynasty. In the water, the middle one is Longtan (Dragon Pond) Pavilion, with Chengxiang (Clear Auspiciousness) Pavilion and Zixiang (Moisture Fragrance) Pavilion on the left and Yongrui (Gushing Luck) Pavilion and Fucui (Floating Green) Pavilion on the right. The five pavilions are linked by S-shaped flat bridges that look like a crouching dragon, hence the name. They are the oldest pavilion group in the imperial gardens (II-7-4a,b,c).

On the south-north Nine-bend Bridge on Lesser Ying Islet in West Lake, Hangzhou, are five pavilions, linked by winding flat bridges which run through Central Islet, totaling 300 m in length. Different in shape, size and position, these five pavilions are connected by bridges, a consummate achievement in the pavilion arts. Standing in any of the five pavilions, one has a beautiful view of the three ponds (II-7-5a,b,c).

A Five-pavilion Bridge can be found over Star Lake in Zhaoqing, Guangdong and over Slim West Lake in Yangzhou. The Five-pavilion Bridge on the Star Lake stretches into the water, with a distance of 10 m between two pavilions. The one in the center is an octagonal pavilion with double eaves; and the other four have hipped

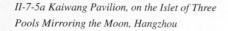

II-7-5a Kaiwang Pavilion, on the Islet of Three Pools Mirroring the Moon, Hangzhou

II-7-5b Tingtingting Pavilion, on the Islet of Three Pools Mirroring the Moon, Hangzhou

II-7-5c The Pavilion of Complete Rapport on the Islet of Three Pools Mirroring the Moon, Hangzhou

II-7-6 Front view of five pavilions in a residential area in Beijing

and pointed tops in the shape of a cross. Standing in the pavilions, visitors will be very close to the water. The Five-pavilion Bridge over the Slim West Lake is located on a lotus-flower earth dyke, the five pavilions linked with each other as a whole. The bridge piers are high. The bridge has 15 arches; it is said that when the moon is bright, people can see the reflections of the moon from each opening .

In the courtyard of a residential quarter for the staff of a certain university in Beijing stand five pavilions, one in the middle and the other four on the four corners. These five pavilions are linked by canopies and can be reached by a cross path. Between late spring and early summer

every year, the canopies are covered with fragrant Chinese wisteria flowers. The central courtyard also has evergreen cedars and bushes, offering a green environment for staff (II-7-6).

In summary, no matter whether a group of pavilions consists of several independent structures, or an integral whole linked by corridors and bridges, China's pavilion art has unquestionably attained a very high level. Modern pavilion groups have greatly changed in shape and usage in accordance with actual needs. Some pavilion groups are used as public waiting halls or restaurants; only their roofs distinguish them as pavilions.

III. Examples of Pavilion Parks

As mentioned above, almost all parks and gardens in China include pavilions. Moreover, pavilions are very rich in art and culture. Nevertheless, it is rare for one park to contain a wide variety of pavilions.

East Lake Park in Fengxiang County, Shaanxi Province and Taoranting (Pavilion of Happiness and Ease) Park in Beijing are representative of parks with many ancient and modern pavilions, each with its own unique characteristics. East Lake Park, built by Su Dongpo, a great scholar of the Song Dynasty (960—1279), features profound cultural connotations of pavilion culture. Over the past several thousand years, pavilions in the park have been destroyed, but now we can still see the traces of the layout and conception of the ancient pavilions. Taoranting in Beijing reflects modern people's creativity in their study of China's traditional pavilion culture, a development well received by society. Hence these two parks are the representatives of ancient and modern pavilion cultures. They are worth studying.

1. The East Lake Park of Fengxiang in Shaanxi—A Representative Pavilion Park of Ancient China

Lying to the east of the old city of Fengxiang County, Shaanxi Province, East Lake Park was first constructed in the seventh year of the Jiayou reign of Emperor Renzong (1062) of the Song Dynasty, with a history of nearly 1,000 years. Though the park was renovated several times during later dynasties, the basic layout and architecture was virtually unchanged since the Song Dynasty. The positions and foundations of the buildings, pavilions, and terraces, are all the same as they were then. It is probably the oldest preserved urban park in China.

Su Dongpo, an eminent writer of the Song Dynasty, went to Fengxiang to serve as an aide to the prefect in charge of the local government archives at the age of 26. Su Dongpo found a clear pool in the east of the city, and he ordered a lake dug there that was filled with water from Phoenix Spring. He planted willow trees and built pavilions by the lake, and grew lotus flowers in the lake, thus creating a beautiful garden where people could enjoy themselves. Farmers could also irrigate their fields with water from the lake. This lake lies in the east of the city, hence the name.

From that time on, a large number of scholars of past ages visited the park, writing many poems in praise of

A Sketch of East Lake

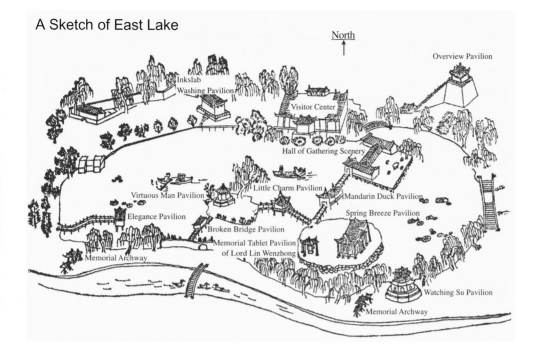

North

Overview Pavilion

Inkslab
Washing Pavilion

Visitor Center

Hall of Gathering Scenery

Little Charm Pavilion

Virtuous Man Pavilion

Mandarin Duck Pavilion

Spring Breeze Pavilion

Elegance Pavilion

Broken Bridge Pavilion

Memorial Tablet Pavilion
of Lord Lin Wenzhong

Memorial Archway

Watching Su Pavilion

Memorial Archway

Inkslab Washing Pavilion, Scenery Collection Pavilion, Mandarin Duck Pavilion, Spring Breeze Pavilion, Watching Su Pavilion, Broken Bridge Pavilion, Little Charm Pavilion, and Light Admiration Pavilion (III-1-1 to III-1-11).

The pavilions are different in their positions, shapes and implications. Happy Rain Pavilion and Appropriation Pavilion on Lingxu Terrace have been famous since ancient China. Most of them were constructed in the Song Dynasty, and the rest were built in the Qing Dynasty and the Republic of China period, in addition to a few new ones built recently. Hence the East Lake Park is the oldest pavilion park in China.

We can see the cultural characteristics of East Lake Park through an examination of Happy Rain Pavilion.

A rectangular structure, Happy Rain Pavilion sits on a one-meter-high terrace, with 12 pillars and a gable roof.

the scenery of East Lake. Of the poems handed down, about one-third sing the praises of the pavilions in the park. In addition to poems there are also essays eulogizing the lake. This demonstrates the importance of pavilions to East Lake Park.

With an area of 14 hectares, East Lake Park is divided into inner and outer lake zones. Except for the lake and open grass, the park is mainly occupied by pavilions, of which nearly 20 have been restored, such as Virtuous Man Pavilion, Happy Rain Pavilion, Appropriation Pavilion, Jade Water Pavilion, Overview Pavilion,

III-1-1 Happy Rain Pavilion

A stone tablet stands in the center of the pavilion, with an inscription: "Remember Happy Rain Pavilion." Originally this pavilion was located to the northeast of Fengxiang Prefecture, but it was later moved to East Lake. The inscription records why this pavilion got this name.

In the sixth year of the Jiayou reign of Emperor Renzong (1061) of the Song Dynasty, Su Dongpo came to Fengxiang to take up an official post. In the following year he ordered a pavilion be constructed to the north of his office. To the south of the pavilion, a pond was dug, from which he fetched water for trees. That spring, a drought occurred, with no rainfall for an entire month. Everyone was worried, but Su Dongpo and the prefect prayed for rain several times. Sure enough, a miraculous rain followed that even cured sick people of their illnesses. The people all rejoiced. At this time, the pavilion was completed. A banquet was thrown at the pavilion, at which Su Dongpo vividly expounded how important rainfall was to the people, believing that rain could grant happiness. He also suggested the newly built pavilion be named "Happy Rain Pavilion" to commemorate the joyous event.

The historical records and the features of the existing pavilions in the East Lake Park reveal the following characteristics about the park:

First, as most of the area of East Lake Park is covered by water, most pavilions in the park are related to water. Some sit in the lake, some stand on bridges, and the others lie by the lake. The pavilions and water plants complement each other, creating an elegant and charming scene.

Second, located in the east of the city, East Lake Park is an ideal place for visitors to appreciate the setting sun, sunset glows, and nightfall mist. An old saying goes: "The sun sets in front of the Happy Rain Pavilion," recognizing the perfect combination of pavilions and nature.

Third, the names of the pavilions in the East Lake Park reflect major events with deep cultural connotations, such as Happy Rain Pavilion and Virtuous Man Pavilion. As the oldest existing pavilion park in China, the East Lake is a precious heritage worth studying.

III-1-2 The Broken Bridge seen from the door of Phoenix Drinking Pond

III-1-4a Interior of Broken Bridge Pavilion

III-1-3 Appropriation Pavilion on Linxu Terrace

III-1-4b A distant view of the Broken Bridge

III-1-5 The front view of the "Untied Boat" in East Lake

III-1-7 Watching Su Pavilion

III-1-6 Mandarin Duck Pavilion
(commemorating Su Dongpo and his wife)

III-1-8 Spring Breeze Pavilion

III-1-9 Virtuous Man Pavilion

III-1-10 Inkslab Washing Pavilion

III-1-11 Overview Pavilion

2. The Hundred-Pavilion Garden of Taoranting in Beijing—A Typical Example of Pavilion Parks in Modern China

Taoranting Park in Beijing is a large park constructed in the early years of the People's Republic of China. In the southwestern part of Taoranting Park, several dozen pavilions have been built, forming the Garden of China's Famous Pavilions (III-2-1 to III-2-9). With an area of 10 hectares, this rare high-quality cultural garden links history and culture with amusement, popularizing history and culture, and promoting China's time-honored pavilion culture.

Since China's adoption of open door reforms, pavilion parks have sprung up like mushrooms in China, such as the Hundred Pavilion Park in Hengdian, Dongyang City, Zhejiang Province; the Hundred Pavilion Amusement Park in Beijing and Pavilion Garden on Mount Jiugong in Hubei Province.

Though there are thousands of pavilions throughout China, the ones represented in the Garden of China's Famous Pavilions are the most exquisite and culturally significant. Before its construction, architects thoroughly analyzed and researched the shapes and layout of the pavilions. They follow the following principles in the building of parks of famous pavilions:

1) "Spare no effort to retain original features." A famous pavilion's cultural connotation and form are of great

III-2-1b The Alone Sober Pavilion is named for a famous line from Qu Yuan: "Everybody is drunk; I alone am sober."

III-2-2 An imitation of Little Orchid Pavilion in Shaoxing

historical value. Therefore, every effort must be made to preserve the original features.

2) "Create an environment like the original in spirit." Over a long process of history virtually all famous pavilions have been destroyed and rebuilt many times. It is almost impossible to rebuild pavilions in their exact places and environments. In a modern pavilion park, many pavilions must be built in a zone of about 10 hectares, each in an environment resembling the original.

3) "Attach importance to happiness and ease." The Garden of China's Famous Pavilions in Taoranting Park represents happiness and ease. Moreover, famous pavilions were constructed by intellectuals from the Spring and Autumn and Warring States Periods to the Qing Dynasty when the feudal age ended, a period of more than 3,000 years. The pavilions in the garden were constructed according to descriptions by scholars of various ages, representing profound cultural connotations and making visitors happy and carefree.

III-2-3 An imitation of Goose Pond in Shaoxing

III-2-4 An imitation of the Cottage Pavilion of Du Fu (712−770) in Chengdu

III-2-5 The Moonlit Pavilion, named for a line from the Song of the Pipa (a type of lute) by the poet Bai Juyi (772−846)

III-2-6 An imitation of Gentle Waves Pavilion in Suzhou

III-2-8 An Immitation of Baipo Pavilion

III-2-7 Drunken Man's Pavilion

III-2-9 The Second Spring Under Heaven Tablet Pavilion

IV. Postscript

Because of my love of the subject, I have been studying and collecting materials on pavilions for years. In the past 10-odd years, I have taken nearly 1,000 photographs of pavilions. I once held a one-man exhibition of photos titled "Pavilion Art" in cooperation with my friends at the Hong Kong Culture Center, and wrote several thousand words of accompanying notes.

I majored in gardening in college. Pavilions cannot be separated from gardens and vice versa. Because of my work, I paid much attention to the shapes and functions of pavilions over many years; and because of my interest in literature, I have naturally studied the written pavilion culture, including the names of pavilions, horizontal inscribed boards, couplets written on scrolls and hung on the pillars of a pavilion, and pavilion notes. I deeply feel that though pavilions are small, they represent profound implications. The pavilion culture is a beautiful flower in the garden of Chinese culture and civilization.

Here I would like to express my heartfelt gratitude to the Foreign Languages Press, especially to Mr. Wang Zhi, an editor there. It is due to their efforts that I have this chance to share my love for pavilions with you, the reader. I also would like to thank Mr. Zhu Dan, an old friend, and Professor Liu Erming of the Architecture Department of Shenzhen University who provided me with relevant materials and helped me with ink sketches.

Because of limited space, I can only present readers with this 24mo picture album, which regrettably covers only a small part of the pavilion culture and does not cover modern pavilions at all. I completed the text and selected the photographs in a two-week period. If there are any errors and careless omissions, please let me know.

Zhu Junzhen, professor of Qinghua University